Ghostlier Demarcations

Ghostlier Demarcations

Poems by

Richard Stuecker

Cover by Shay Culligan
Cover illustration by artist Rex Lagerstrom.

ISBN: 978-1-63980-095-7

Kelsay Books
502 South 1040 East, A-119
American Fork, Utah 84003
Kelsaybooks.com

As always, Barbara

Acknowledgments

A number of journals have been kind enough to publish poems included in this book. These include:

Birmingham Arts Review: "Mother's Day."

Broadkill Review: "Rothko On."

Courtship of Winds, District Lit: "Holy Week."

Former People Journal: "Assumption Day,"

Main Street Rag: "Espresso Amaro."

Otherwise Engaged: A Literature and Arts Journal: "Cave Hill Cemetery," "Mother's Day," "Only Child."

October Hill: "Everything Dies."

Pif: "Lucky Stone."

Poesis Literary Review: "Strawberry Moon," (reprint), "Everything Dies" (reprint)

Poetica: "Evening Walks (part one)"

West Trade Review: "A Single Rose Unfurls."

WMWJ: "Strawberry Moon."

The following poems were included in the chapbook *The Uncertainty Principle* published by Kelsay Books in 2020: "Assumption Day," "Caffeine Lingers," "Chartres," "Devilish," "Espresso Amaro," "Evening Walks (parts one and two)," "Near Occasions of Sin."

Thanks to B.J. Wilson, The Bluegrass Writers Studio, many friends and members of the Louisville writers community who have supported my work through personal encouragement and at readings such as the Flying Out Loud reading series hosted by Steve Cambron and the BGWS readings at Eastern Kentucky University.

Contents

Rothko On

The maker's rage to order words of the sea,
Words of the fragrant portals, dimly-starred,
And of ourselves and of our origins,
In ghostlier demarcations, keener sounds.

—Wallace Stevens, *The Idea of Order at Key West*

Strawberry Moon

Escape from the black cloud that surrounds you,
Then you will see your own light as radiant as
the full moon.

—Rumi

Evening Walks

1.

An urgent wind thrusts us
relents an occasional pause
to our daily walk. Not knowing
what might blow in,
our faulty pace quickens us
to remember much we lost
that meant everything once,
now flutter, swirl, vanish
into the moonless sky.
Turning back, we always turn
toward where we come from,
against chill reminiscence
rising less and less, more and more
we lock the door to still the night.

2.

Walking under shivering oaks,
saplings in the '30s, now giants,
I wonder, as they sway
before the storm coming,
if they fear for themselves, as lately
they seem to be taken one by one,
having so long flexed and swirled
but stood their ground?
Only last October they glorified the fall,
more brilliant than any year in memory.
Now, stark December, only the oaks
resist dropping withered leaves.

Maples, elms, dogwoods, ashes make
barren forms against the snow-filled clouds,
allowing us to track the falcon that moved in
last spring and the waning moon that
hid all summer. This storm may twist
them until they crack or uproot,
fallen trunks as tall as I am walking by.

3.

Often, we talk more
when we walk under
oaks at last turning
our attention toward
winter—more than when
we sit by an empty fireplace
late in the evening—lately
I've been reading novels
I read when I learned
to love reading—Poe,
Hawthorne, Bronte, du Maurier—
gothic secrets hidden behind walls,
locked doors, fireplaces.
Threatening weather, wind
tearing dry leaves from branches
pushes us homeward, driving our
thoughts, reminiscences, fears.
A good night to fire up
some logs, recline back with
a book that chills my soul,
again the joy of reading words before
I learned to parse texts, deconstruct,
images of moors, mad men, specters
animating my brain.

A Single Rose Unfurls

A single rose unfurls,
harbinger of a sudden
explosion of blossoms.
After a warm winter
unable to kill the herbs
we snip into our soups,
we eat salads on the deck
within a garden I built
to recover from a sickness
that nearly took me.

During our evening walks,
neighbors whose names
we barely know burst from
their homes sudden as an iris
in full flag, shouting greetings
as though we were emerging
celebrities, taking a victory lap.

Before, we only passed fellow dwellers
in this bungalow community
in cars, waving to thank us
for letting them go first,
on our way out to the city,
to theaters now dark, restaurants,
curbside pickup only, empty
parking lots once filled
with anxious drivers
vying for up close parking.

On evening walks, I rediscover
where I live, whom I live among,
finding a connection I had forgotten,
once suspicious about who votes for whom,
who might be carriers of some dread.
Now the dread is here full blown.
Along the way azaleas riot under
tulip poplars, blooming cherries, we
walk until the first star of evening
appears in a sky fading into icy darkness,
revealing tonight a starry cosmos.

Cave Hill Cemetery

At noon,
through massive iron gates
we move at funeral speed,
escaping for a moment
our quarantined homes away
from the plague-filled city—
into a necropolis of long shadows thrust
from ancient oaks, hickories, hemlocks:
where dogwoods explode a thousand
white crosses and redbuds sprout purple,
as if at once these trees were resurrecting,
burgeoning life against a sky so blue
the sun dances between sudden, alive branches,
carrying with us a shudder, a fear of dying,
too soon, alone.

Lithe runners, jogging the sides of twisting
black driveways, pace the movement while
we idle to read and remember inscriptions
on stone monuments recording longevity,
sometimes fate: a sudden cough of blood,
doomed heart attack, Spanish flu,
crib death, drunken accident, a life
self-taken, a summer drowning. A
laughing child squirms away giggling,
escaping her father. Who wouldn't
run toward flowering life under
drooping vines of blue moon wisteria?
Graves await the mounting dead, from
breath stolen by a handshake,
a forgotten encounter, a crowded dinner,
the greeter at the church door, smiling,
inviting the disease into unwary lungs.

Away from our drear homes, anxious
among memories recorded in rows,
no one can remember these dead lying
under Victorian carved splendor,
near an amphitheater in an arboretum,
where bands once played, where once
the living washed gravestones and picnicked
as old soldiers spoke to rows of soldiers
taken by skirmish and clash.
Now fresh graves lie waiting for new deaths,
racers rush against what may come
even to the young, surely to those who are not.
A single red tulip stands, the color of a poppy
pinned to a mourning suit on Veterans Day.
Even a cemetery drive is a risk for us, forbidden
yet, confined for days we journey out,
embracing a cold spring, passing back through the
gated entry, into an empty city, once alive.

April, 2020

I shutter the windows at night,
slant them open in sunshine, day breaks,
some days seem like summer, others
Eliot cruel, the long wait, contained by
house, garden, neighborhood. The garden
has never seen so much attention.
Digging weeds, transplanting renewal
for a future spring in beds I forgot
all last year. A hawk hovers against
angry April clouds holding back rain,
thunderclaps, lightning streak, a torrent.

On the street, our grandsons whizz
by on bikes, they circle us,
as though we are prey. In our treed
neighborhood under massive oaks
dripping rain still, planted long
before I was born, we explore our
perimeter, waving to neighbors we
have not met, smiling from
across the street, no one stops
to talk anymore, they have babies,
when did they move in? Where did
our old parishioners go? When did they
slip away? Slanting the shutter to see
the hawk hang low over rooftops,
vigilant for what may come,
what might go, I turn on the lights,
each one in the living room,
so we might read, ponder and pray.

A Single Clap

A single clap,
releases an avalanche,
frees an ovation,
the fuse spark travelling
up the snow bound
mountain, the fall
of rock and ice,
the audience stands
applauds standing until
the curtain falls.

Who heard the clap,
when your pistol shot
the bullet into your heart?

Did you not see the signs
of renewal everywhere you
looked? Even as your dark
night fell, the curtain falling
like the pall on the casket
over you, over us all.

Reverberations travel,
a clap of thunder spreads
after a shock of light
splits a tree in two. At last,
spring rains quench
parched winter soil.

Mother's Day

Hugging mother is like hugging a lobster,
all hard shell and sharp pincers. I am
her only son, her project, her ambition.
Age 95—she called 15 times in a row
last night, every three minutes, at 4 a.m.
I gotta get out of here. Locked up in room 311,
locked in by Covid-19. *I want a lobster roll
from the Lobster Hut down at Plymouth.*

I escaped to Hingham once, where there were
plenty of lobsters, 1200 miles from home.
She called, *Your father is dying.*
In my memory lurks a lobster bake in
my New England cousin's back yard,
digging a pit, ocean water, seaweed, clams.
Sometimes I stop by Kroger's, bring home a pair,
boil them in a steamer, crack open their shells
dig out the sweet meat inside. On Mother's Day
I crack open her heart, pick out whatever sweetness
I find there, landlocked in Kentucky, we both erode
like granite lining the North Atlantic shore.

Strawberry Moon

Under a burgeoning sun, I clear out places
to let flowering vines thrive, climb
a wooden trellis. Day casts light that kills
viruses, as well as it casts shadows,
where vermin hide.

A boy—perhaps a girl—
has snatched a nest, cardinal or robin?
The remains of eggs, woven sticks strewn
across the sidewalk in front of my house
I swept just yesterday. Perhaps it belonged
to the robin that gobbled a green lizard
before it could dig back in its hole, save itself.
On the porch, passive, I sip an espresso.
paranoia, terror, outrage seem everywhere.
Wild strawberries ripen under the bulging moon.

Lucky Stone

Sometimes I smell mildew and pine.
I know it is my grandmother.
I am again awakened by lace curtains
touching my face, breeze blown through
a screen, through a screen where I see
a dirt path wander into the woods,
a gravel drive, wooden garage where her
Chevy waits to be driven. When she
pulls the doors open, the smell of oil,
gasoline, sawdust, age; she opens the door,
so I can jump in and sit beside her, just
she and me, while the others sleep. Down
Wooded Hill and across the Four Corners,
past Saint Andrews and its fine steeple,
the red brick school house across from the
high school toward the North River Bridge,
through Norwell to the rotary, where the sky
opens up to the sea and gulls call above a row
of shops and cafes and book stores to the point
where the lighthouse stands, has stood at the
Atlantic shore through fogs and storms
and ages of lovers, sun burnt families who
take the same cabins each year, at Scituate. We pull up
where we always pull up to and sit on the bench
we always sit on, out of her purse she hands me
a wrapped in waxed paper piece of salt water
taffy. We suck on and chew and chew on
our thoughts until we search for a lucky stone,
granite wrapped by a white line, on the rocky beach,
storm-tossed smooth. I keep one she finds
in my pocket, always have, to touch, to feel,
to remember who I am and where I come from.

Blue Heron

Last weekend a Blue Heron
flew over our roof on its way,
who knows where, in this urban
landscape, surely not over to the
jetport where a million packages fly over
our house every morning at 4 a. m.
Harbinger of sequester
in my house, my garden, my front lawn?
Or a salve to ease my nerves, I am so jittery
and anxious being vulnerable—or is it expendable?
A prophet of change, something of the spirit?

I remember seeing one in the stream
behind your home where you once saved a beaver
from a neighbor's chain link fence. We sit
face to face in our masks, on a cool spring night
as the first fireflies rise out of the grass.
I feel a draw to wild birds as my life grows
simple, more fragile. Death quickens my search
for connection to compassion: all in this moment
a possibility, a promise to lift us like blue herons,
wide wings spread against the sun.

Everything Dies

Everything dies,
nothing returns as it was.
Even the perennials
now wilt in my garden,
turn to dust, will only return
as similes of what was in the spring.
Snake-like in among the dying weeds
and blooms I twist and turn and
leave my skin behind. It is another
season, after season, after season,
Will there be another?
Or will I turn my garden
over to another gardener,
who turns the earth over into his own,
no longer even a simile of mine?
Or will winter be the end of it?
Or will new owners turn
this ground into something other than a garden?

Everything lives,
as though renewal will renew
what has always been, a metaphor
of living, a mirror of past seasons,
when, what was, was; what is, is:
will not be again exact, even if intention
wills it or even if we might long for it
again, believing we can revive
what was into new life. It will be
new life, perhaps familiar, perhaps similar
but ever evolving like garments
we wear to the sea, fashionable
this season, but antique in the next.

Full of hope I sprinkle ashes left
by my parents into the soil of my garden,
turning over layers, blending what was
with what is, believing that what will be
will be but a shadow of what I intended.

My Mother Slips into the Mystery

There is a hush as though
we are entering a convent
at morning prayer. Footsteps
scuffle down hallways,
nuns' feet on their way to chapel,
but these are nurses and aides.

6 a.m. The call that came
awakened us from our personal
myths, night dream journeys.
The door buzzer alarmed us
the reality of death.
Corvid-19 has slithered
into the nursing home.

Two nurses vest us in plastic,
hooded albs, gloves, surgical masks.
The body of my mother
lies flat against white sheets,
her head buried in a pillow,
eyes closed, shallow breathing.
I question the nurse with my eyes:
"How long?" She whispers,
"It could be any time, probably today,
tonight, possibly tomorrow."
She brings us tea, packs of cookies
crackers we will not eat.
She strokes my mother's hair:
"It's okay, baby. It's okay".

My wife and I sit at the base
of the bed in metal folding chairs.
Books, all the library books,

are gone from the shelves
the many books she loved,
forgot she read, read again retaining
what she read only as she read them.
Gone. The room mostly empty,
save the art, a Jamie Wyeth print
of a hunting dog; a water color
of a lighthouse, pictures and cards
her grandchildren made tucked in frames.
Her clothes folded in drawers,
Cosmetics, junk jewelry, an empty envelope.

Mother is a bird, tucked up into her nest.
She has no weight, having only eaten
ice cream and nibbles of pureed food
for at least half a year. Skeletal,
her skin dry and thin as onionskin paper
my father used to make copies
in his manual typewriter. It is a shock
since we haven't seen her since January.

I think I should light a candle, maybe two,
maybe two long tapers and a crucifix
on the table where the books have vanished.
I remember the Catholic sick call set
with its beeswax candles and crucifix
tucked away in a steamer trunk,
put away in the basement
of the house they lived together in
for over fifty years.

She will be cremated, my father's
ashes mixed by their son with hers,
taken to Scituate, her New England home,
scattered to the wind and sea.

The black woman in white,
angelic care-giver, from time to time
looks in, again touches her hair,
pats my wife's shoulder leaves
without a word, but leaves a smile
as she goes, closing the heavy oak door.

We move the chairs up next to her on
either side. Simultaneously we take her hands,
feel the life within them. There is strength
left yet so we know that she can hear
and understand. I think of every prayer
I can draw out of the well of my Catholic past
prayers the Ursuline sisters drilled
year after year. Without beads I pray
rosary after rosary. In silence.
Each of us take turns reminding her
that we love her. That it is okay for her to go.
To let go. That she is safe and
it is time to slip out of her tired body.
Over and over, I pray the Hail Marys
Glory Be's, Our Fathers on my fingers.

"You can see in her limbs how the blood
is collecting," says the nurse. "It won't be long now."
It is not long. My wife says: "I think she is gone."

I look over quickly at her face
she has stopped breathing. Her head
moves quickly, almost violently,
from one side to the other in a final
"No" to death, and she is gone.
Her mouth frozen in a perfect O.
The nurse re-appears as though we have called her.
She listens to her heart.
"Take your time," she says,
"there is no rush." But we
do not wait. I look at her face again.
There is no one there.

Chartres

Longing for pilgrimage:
the quiet and simple, even
among the throngs; I am
unfit to walk the Camino Santiago,
it does not draw me
as does Notre Dame de Chartres,
the Madonna in her celestial space
built of stone and story in the windows.

Longing to surrender to clarity,
to empty my vessel, fill my void
with completeness gained by
falling deep into the abyss of love,
endless embrace, no expectation or
understanding, seeking the eternal
connection your builders sought
constructing your earthly home.

Longing to enter into the sacred blue light,
believe like common artisans
within the stone silence buttressed
by faith, walk the labyrinth
to the center of transformation
not to perfection, to be comforted,
my heart touched by the warmth of grace,
the Mother's kiss soothing my lost self.

The Apotheosis of Sister Raymounda

O, necessary sin of Adam . . . O happy fault . . .
　　　　　　　　　　　　　—Easter Proclamation

Holy Week

1.
(Fellini footage/Nino Roto score)

Predictable piazza du Padova.
A ragged figure purses lips
to a silver mouthpiece, lifts
a haunting anthem skyward,
stars tumble enchantment.
White powder drifts from
drooping clown's mouth,
precise steps, ring enscribed,
impossible feats unveiled,
applause, dispensed
crowd disperses.

(fade to black)

2.
Sister Raymunda fingers colored chalks
        only sainted nuns may touch,
                angels, flaming colors
                        of the Cirque du Monte Carlo,
                                across a scarred blackboard, choirs
                                        swirling around the eye of
                        God
                                within a sky of Giotto blue.
                She reveals to our amazement:
                        Il Paradiso —

Sister Raymunda (who has never studied Dante, in Italian nor in
translation) blazes Wonder:

Some of you may squeeze into
the celestial mystery with the
grace of a street urchin,
if you are skilled and scourged.
Sadly, most will find yourself
drudging in the icy pits.

Before us, swirling fingers,
      on another slate rises leviathan Satan,
           gorging sinners as blinded Polyphemus
              swallowed drunken sailors
                    before their fellows fled his cave
                       under the bellies of bleating
          sheep.

        Jesus, remember me when you come into
    your kingdom

              Her apotheosis:
              Sister drifts across the room,
              brandishes a long oak pointer,
              a black garbed Seraph taps
              each stunned head,
              transforms us into song birds:
                       cardinals,
                       bluebirds,
                       crows.

3.
Palm Sunday, my brother-in-law decided
to die a long slow death
on his family room floor.

Days passed.
A tiny car appeared expelling
A doctor, a nurse, a lady
(with an alligator purse)
plied their instruments, found no remedy.
Weeks passed.
Tony stared ceaselessly
through a stately window:
a gnarly dogwood tree —
the wood of the Cross —
buds and blossoms
ten thousand crucifixions.

4.
   Sunset at Scituate, clownish clouds
       tumble toward nighttime, radiant stars.
                A school of young sailors
                    follow a schooner,
            haul in their sails.
       A cormorant dives deep for fish.

I sit on a bench my grandmother sat upon, pregnant with
my mother, unmarried,
      searching

            below the stalwart lighthouse
            seagull cries divert my thoughts
            toward fluttering canvas across the
                      point

a painted elephant announces:

Under the Big Top—as the circus should be
seen!

(Tonight. I will snake my body into the death-defying show)

Maternity in the Children's Ward

When I was three years old,
my mother lied, maternity
not her long suit, telling me
she would stay all night
with me at the hospital, when
in the night I screamed for her,
her chair empty, the room dark
the heavy door closed until
a dark figure, a nun
her starched wimple leaned
over my mouth and her mouth
whispered *Your mother has left,*
now pee in this jug and stop
this noise or I'll give you
something to scream about.
I dropped the metal jug
Sister Mary Raymunda
pulling me from the crib,
my pee splashing
the bed and floor.

Only Child

When I was a child,
Sister Raymunda regaled
our fifth grade, telling
the story of Thomas a'Kempis,
buried alive, exhumed,
his coffin found with claw marks
on his coffin lid. Denying
him sainthood. Well,
I am no saint, and have often
awakened screaming, clawing
at my sheets and blankets.
I know confinement well,
the searing gaze of parents
on their only child,
disappointing their dreams,
entrapped in thought, word and deed,
escaping into sin, (thank you again,
Sister Raymunda
for your excellent instruction
on the nature of sin!)
only for a time, always
the fate of only children to come home,
serve their aging parents,
bury them alone, in a field nearby.

Autoimmune

Where is Jesus when you need him least? Up in heaven giving you grief.
Where is Jesus when you need him most? Playing cards with the Holy Ghost.
                                                    —Sister Raymunda

No, no deity would be so cruel,
or vengeful as you seem to be,
my body, attacking me
taking one organ at a time.

What pissed you off, anyway?
Wasn't aging enough for you?
Creeping weakness over time,
dry skin pulled over bones,

creaking, joints aching
all night, fingers stiffen
half sleep, half awake
self-anger over remembrance

of what might have been
could have been then
should have been if only
I ought to have been other?

It was you all the time,
snaking through my organs,
first thyroid then kidney
then bladder infection after infection,

Scope after scope while
I wet myself, lose control
of bowels, sudden black outs
falling whenever I lean over.

43

Well, I've had enough of
hospital trips, sweet nurses,
pricks in my arm, slow drips
a pick up my dick so I can piss.

Jesus, finish your game,
sweep down your chariot,
kiss my lips with the fire
of your flaming tongue.

Questions for Sister Raymunda

Must I meet everyone I knew alive? Indifferent parents who not
    once hugged or kissed me? The All-American all us boys
    were compared with? The coach who checked us out in the
    showers, the piano teacher whose hand slid up my thigh?
    The chick who made sure all her girlfriends knew I called
    her for a date and believed she was washing her hair? The
    jerks from SAE who called me a queer every afternoon
    when they sat on their bench rating women one to ten: slut
    to bitch? The drunk fullback who beat me up for the hell of
    it?

When we resurrect, must I keep this same body, the one no one
    noticed, that made the team but sat on the bench, that failed
    to score the winning goal, that never was fit, that lusted
    after both sexes, remained faithful to one? Condemned by
    the other?

Will we really live-in mansions? MacMansions? Peons on a
    celestial estate?

Will there be classes? Cults? Envy? Proletariat, Aristocrats, status
    among Saints? Choirs of Angels? Apostles? Disciples?
    Clergy? Popes? Christians? Jews? Jen? Zen? Buddhists?
    All the splintered Baptists? Meditators? Procrastinators?
    Lapsed? Non-believers? Never believers?

Are lepers allowed?

Does Limbo exist? Purgatory? Hell? If so, how come?

If Jesus was human, did he lust? Find faults in himself? Others?
    Angst as an adolescent? Tell dirty jokes? Have any buds
    before the Apostles and the Disciples? Date Mary
    Magdalene? John? Both?

Will I be a sheep or goat and how come goats are less than sheep?

Should I believe the priest who said if I did not tell I would be
saved?

What if, as Sister Raymunda said, we would sing and praise God
all day and night for eternity? Will there be day and night?
Won't that be exhausting?

Do I want to go? Can I chose to be dust? Drop into an ocean's
depths?

Or will there be only love? And Graeter's Raspberry Chocolate
Chip served on Sundays?

The Cogitations of Sister Raymounda

Sister Raymounda awaits at the corner Sister Chrysantha;
      together they sway, their long beads like pendula,
      measure the universe, its constellations, its confirmations,

mysteries of a silent God, on a cold night in November, while the
      wind whips their whimples, they whisper their office,
      together embrace a long-ago travesty jolting a pagan world.

The spires of Saint Pancras pierce burgeoning grey, bare down
      at the black-clad daughters of Ursula, last of their order,
      pacing their prayers while a blue moon arises.

So much to consider, so much to lament, so much to release while
      the planet turns once again away from a world so defined
      one could find redemption on the rubric faith.

Rain, Sister. A torrent, I think. Both wrapping their heads with
      woolen cloaks, they consider the clouds, the street light,
      shadows cast off graffiti marred walls.

The planet flies slowly, the universe whirls, doubt burgeons,
      confusion reigns, ambiguous solutions appear to
      questions the holy sisters can no longer answer.

Espresso Amaro

The voodoo priest and all his powders were as nothing compared to espresso, cappuccino, and mocha, which are stronger than all the religions of the world combined, and perhaps stronger than the human soul itself.

—Mark Helprin

Black as the devil, hot as hell, pure as an angel, sweet as love.

—Charles Maurice de Talleyrand

Near Occasions of Sin

Espresso in a cup lifted
from the Café Chiado,
rich, bitter, darkness
reminiscent of the deep
pleasure taken engaging
in so many delicious sins
described delicately by
my parish priest's sermons.
Partaking of so many of the fruits,
trees of knowledge, plunging
into sweet, idyllic, oblivion,
identifying bad companions,
Near occasions of sin, thank you
Sister Raymounda, for directing me,
instructing me, your guidance
to real life, where I suffer pain,
satisfaction of work. Ecstatic,
profound, enlightening moments,
the final embrace of the Angel of Death.

Caffeine Lingers

Espresso brewed in an
Italian maker traveled
from a bin at the
Mercato di Lucca
in the shade of the wall
surrounding the Centro
poured in small cups
stolen from the Café Chiado
in Lisboa, sipped on my porch
this strangely cool morning in
August when temperatures
ought to be scorching.
Your unexpected call
detailing your new life
break dances my heart.
Bitter caffeine lingers, as does
the remnant of the crushed
beans in the bottom of the cup.
A sparrow dips itself into
a chipped porcelain teapot
I refuse to part with as a
tiny lizard explores aging
brickwork needing tuckpointing,
birdsong surrounds, stirring thoughts,
you finding your way away from me.
The morning warms until
I carry my empty cup inside
to rinse out the dregs.

Devilish

Ironic and hypocritical
sipping the best espresso
reading the horrors
in the *Times,*
awaiting a friend,
while children
at the border await
release from cages,
separated from
their mother's breasts,
sipping this bitter brew,
I become aware
how I am dulled by tweets,
sliding into the slough of
my basest self, willing
to justify myself
because the coffee is so damn,
devilishly rich and good.

Espresso Amaro

A dense summer
Cinzano umbrellas'
shadows cast
across wrought iron
lacy tables;
sipping simple
espresso noting
lackadaisical drivers,
stalled at rush hour;
wondering what universe
lies within each driver
what family horror,
what travesty, triumph,
what dull routine,
what plan for later,
yearning; scanning who
in this slanted café
sees me, sees them?

Assumption Day

Regret and reminiscence float over dense August
Like camel-forming clouds, until a crisp day
silences the season with a killing frost.
Sucking into my lungs molds,
the death of flowering weeds,
my dusty garden droops
untended for weeks beyond
the deck rail where I lounge on a chaise lounge—
weather, cool as the Cape in June,
draws me out for a supermarket croissant,
a cup of Keurig Italian Bold, chill
enough to consider a cigarette, I deny
the pleasure and embrace the caffeine.
tasting a bitter coffee.
Mosquitoes nibbling at my sock tops, I
wonder who sits at my table now in Lisbon
at the Café Chiado, greets Vera, sips espresso
savors savory and sweet as the day ahead might be?

Morning Espresso

Cool June morning breeze whiffs
over the porch, clearing my sleepy
head, morning forgiveness during
an epidemic of hatred and blessed
reconciliation: a cardinal, no bigger
than my left hand sits in the grass,
away from its nest in the dogwood.
Already the boys down the street
celebrate the 4th with bangs of
firecrackers and whizzing rockets,
Juneteenth just passed. On my cup
a phoenix emblazoned, dark espresso,
bitter beginning to summer. What
might I say to my grandsons who,
thanks to their fathers have slave blood,
thanks to me have the blood of
commanders in King Phillip's War?
Sounds like gunfire crack the humidity,
thunder boomers coming to drench
us all, announcing the dog days coming.

At Sunergos Café

For B.J.

Surrounded by students,
among roasting aromas,
the swish of steamed milk,
talking poems, checking baristas
as once we might have servers
in bars when undergrads
had we known each other then.
At seventy, I am still shocked
by tattoos on lissome arms,
swank shoulders, muscled necks.
You are half my age yet older
than these scholars, intense in study
or discussing ideas I, too, once
found compelling to the point of death.
Forging a friendship over brews,
the intoxication of poetry, poetics,
cinema, bleak news, bland dreams,
you keep me going forward,
pressing each other to publish,
emmeshed in each other's words
both on the page and spoken.
Breathing in the vitality emitted
from a cacophony of voices,
visions, caffeine and opinion,
the stimulation of both youth
and our conjoined knowledge
I draw into myself renewed life,
the pleasure of our pursuits.

Caffé di Lucca

For BGS

Most days the Keurig—
though we have ditched K-cups
in favor of our own blends—
on this Saint Joseph's day I use
the Italian maker purchased
at the Mercato di Lucca,
first grinding the beans to powder,
the roar of the grinder whirls
a grating noise anticipating brewing,
select a demitasse from the Black Hills—
presidential heads presiding—
rapido water bottom to top,
I snatch the maker just as it
erupts espresso over the burner,
proffer the steaming mixture
to my sleepyhead wife,
this day a croissant with jam,
most days not.

Every Other Thursday

For R.H.

Remind me, how did we become friends?
Oh, yeah, over coffee over at Heine's on
Eastern Parkway. You were full on before
you moved to café au lait, then half-caff
then a firm decision to move from bean to leaf,
before you ordered cappuccino then espresso
straight, not too bitter, with sugar and cream.
I stayed pretty steady with a medium dark roast
and for a while you did as well, for maybe six
months or so then you went small and back again
full on.

It's sometimes like that when you are deciding—
Buy out a business? Pick up a degree?
Marry? No, maybe an ashram on a farm or
just maybe a farm, live in a trailer for a while.
You catalyzed me out of my lethargy, and over
time, I found myself living a notion I had long
considered, but needed a caffeine buzz to realize.

A Bitter Relief

I bring my wife another espresso,
a refill of bitter relief from the chill,
a jolt to quicken our blood while we read,
listen to news of the pandemic.

I watch at the window the passing show
of young couples who have moved into
homes of friends now gone, new lives
commenced in houses built to last a century

or more; bikers taking a last ride before
cold winds blow the fallen leaves adrift
from lawn to lawn, and golden rod peaks its glory:
our spring garden drooping in the chilly air.

Our radio was left by the last owner of our home,
an oakwood console standing on a side wall, refurbed.
Tuning in the news, I wonder who before us listened
to a fireside chat in this room, the stock market plunge?

War news, tornadic weather, ice storms, the end of polio?
The ever-evolving carousel of pop music, jazz, rock, rap?
Who danced on this hardwood floor, or rested on a couch,
entranced by the fire blazing under family portraits?

We have banished TV to other rooms, keeping this
living room pristine to the past, encasing memories
of ourselves and the ghost visions I project upon
these walls, the echoing voices of our children.

Rothko On

What we recall are not memories but old emotions disturbed or resolved—some sense of well-being suddenly shadowed by a cloud—yellow ochres strangely suffused with a drift of gray prevailing over an ambience of rose or the fire diminishing into a glow of embers, or the light when the night descends.
—Duncan Phillips

I'm interested only in expressing basic human emotions—tragedy, ecstasy, doom and so on.
—Mark Rothko

1.National Gallery of Art, May, 1987

After the Calder slowly in motion across the grand entrance, I find the Rothko Room, large canvases on each wall in conversation with one another, colors pulsating in sync.

I stand static as a stabile at their vortex, as though struck by a thunderbolt, no, something more ecstatic, perhaps what saints or repentant sinners feel at the moment of exultation, no exegesis needed.

2. Rothko Room

Inside I feel the sensations I once felt in the Mirror Maze finding myself seeking an ID in the gap before I die, having worn so many faces until now, so many reflections on the walls of glass

a hysteria I felt at the thought I'd never get out, my face over and over just eyes, bodiless, slamming again and again into walls of glass I thought would lead me to freedom, losing myself until at last I stumbled out, into a new life.

3. #10

Rothkos need Rothkos on every wall, each seeking the other, forming a tourbillion, pulling me into my center, like a remembered dream, reminding of a time when I was all together, perhaps on a beach at sunrise, healing light,

the colors of Rothko at dawn, #10, walking with my friend into the sun, when all was possible, life forming, like the curtain rising on a favorite play, leading to an unseen climax, like the climax at the vortex of the Rothko Room.

4. #207

With a friend who jabbers like a tour guide, proud of all things
Toledo, I am suddenly fixed by the Rothko, recently purchased,
singular, lonely, a life seeking culmination toward who I really am,
late Rothko leading toward death, toward a chapel in Houston.

I am a tourist in a life-long search for connection to myself, to others,
like Rothkos in their constant journey from color toward the void,
finding in the paintings an ultimate joy found in deep red sunsets
cooling into blue night, the passage of blue to sleep, to dream.

5. Rothko Chapel

Into the Zen of blackness, into the apse of Good Friday, droning priest, strange melodious candles and incense, altar boys in black cassocks, station to station the death of the Christ, hanging on the tree of life, between earth and heaven, suspended, like a Rothko.

Black is a complete emptiness of color, an abyss, triptychs consume all light in a silence where only breathing is apparent, the journey of us all complete, as Rothko's death, tools of the artist made to gouge out his life in a rectangle of blood.

Go Van Gogh

Cambridge

A dream: The war over. Inside a bunker, afraid to come out. Fearful of being the last ones killed by an unwitting enemy. Casting lots to see who would go out first. I am chosen. Slowly, turning a massive steel wheel and I push out the door. Stepping out, I step into a Van Gogh. Colors alive as a bonfire under midnight stars in the wilderness. Van Gogh vibrant. The vibrancy of souls merging. The vibrancy of a Rothko room. Starry night landscape dissolving into olive trees dissolving into summer day. Fat Van Gogh sun. Lakeside, sitting in samadhi. Still pool reflecting shrubs, purple twisting trees. Green dissolving into Buddha sitting. Living tanghka. Beatific eyes and smile.

Seattle

Museum walk: Up a long staircase past celestial lions, after Chihulilly installations, Van Gogh exhibit stands waiting for me. On the left, Olive Trees. On the right Starry Night. Into the collection, into dreamscape. Van Gogh landscapes, thick paint, fat suns, sunlight of Arles. Sunlight of a Rothko. Morning Carolina coast sunrise. Outside the exhibit, turning, looking up a staircase, Golden Buddha, sitting in serene samadhi. Beatific smile. Leading to the totems of native shamans.

Rembrandt Ramble

The Prodigal Son

Rothko red. Rembrandt red. Red blood draining. Every red drop cleansed during a five hour sit in the dialysis chair. Blood chilling, chilling my blood, coursing in and out of my body. Cleansing. Prodigal red. I have been prodigal in my life. Kneeling before my father, shrouded in red. Begging. Brother sneering at the side. Why should he not? Faithful one. Faith full one. While I wallowed with pigs.

I am my faithful brother. Detached. Pissed. Bedecked. Implacable. Have I not the right? Am I not entitled? Not even a goat given for celebration. I am the fatted calf. Slaughtered. Broiled. Sacrificed. Served for this prodigal. I am the bystanders. Confused by this father. Hanger-on. Parasites.

I am the mother. Weeping behind the curtain. Prayers rising. I am the father. My life given for my sons. Prodigal myself as a young man. Finding compassion for both my sons. Both sons breaking my heart.

Cleansing. Filtering out the impurities of my life. The way of suffering. The way of purification. The way of stillness. Unable to move the length of the cleansing. All around the room my fellow prodigals. My fellow elder brothers. My fellow elders. Community of penitents. Rothko red blood cleansing in the machines. Blood chilling. Chilling our blood. Sitting as one sits in the Rothko room. Seeking. Begging. Feeling. Accepting the compassion of Rothko.

About the Author

Richard Stuecker is a poet and writer who graduated from Duke University in 1970. A Pushcart Prize nominee, he holds an MFA from the Bluegrass Writer's Studio at Eastern Kentucky University. His poems, creative non-fiction, and book reviews have appeared in many national publications. A collection of essays on conscious aging, *Vibrant Emeritus,* was published in 2014 by John Hunt Publishing (London). A chapbook of poems, *The Uncertainty Principle* was published by Kelsay Press in 2020. Ric lives in Louisville, Kentucky with his wife Barbara. When possible, they travel, but mostly they dote on their four grandchildren.